GOD
THE
LOVER
OF YOUR
Soul

Relationship Not Religion

A Guide To Divine Intimacy

HOLLIS C. SPENCE

WESTBOW
P R E S S®
A DIVISION OF THOMAS NELSON
& ZONDERVAN

The intent of this book is to offer information of a general nature to help you in
your quest for emotional and spiritual well-being. In addition to the information
contained in this book, it is always advised to seek sound and adequate
professional help for specific situations (e.g., pastors, Christian counselors).
In the event the information in this book is used for yourself, the author and
the publisher assume no responsibility for your actions and experiences.

WestBow Press books may be ordered through booksellers or by contacting:

WestBow Press
A Division of Thomas Nelson & Zondervan
1663 Liberty Drive
Bloomington, IN 47403
www.westbowpress.com
844-714-3454

Cover Design By:
Panagiotis Lampridis

ISBN: 978-1-6642-2141-3 (sc)
ISBN: 978-1-6642-2143-7 (hc)
ISBN: 978-1-6642-2142-0 (e)

Library of Congress Control Number: 2021901403

Print information available on the last page.

WestBow Press rev. date: 12/16/2021

This book is dedicated to my God (Yahweh), my Savior Jesus (Yeshua), my wife (Katina), and our children. Also, to all the authentic God seekers in the world!

Contact the Author

Hollis C. Spence

2807 Allen Street

(Suite 461)

Dallas, TX 75204

(972) 637-9966

Contact@GodTheLoverOfYourSoul.com

* * *

God loves each of us as if there were only one of us.
—Augustine

God carries your picture in His wallet.
—Tony Campolo

Contents

Introduction

Have you ever had those moments when you think, *There has to be more than this? God, where are you?* Have you ever had those secret, unshared moments of disconnect with God, challenging your beliefs and asking, "God, why can't I feel you?" This book is designed to bring clarity to all those unsettling questions. I clearly understand this aspect of your spiritual and emotional journey, with your soul declaring, "There must be more to this. There just has to be more than this!" I believe God puts in us the desire to know him more intimately, whether it is dormant or active. As declared in the book of Psalms, "He shall give thee the desires of thine heart" (Psalm 37:4 KJV). That desire for intimacy is satisfied only by the experience. If that is true naturally, it is true spiritually. By reading this book, you will be able to learn how to remove the religious imagery of God that has hindered you from experiencing a more intimate connection with the lover of your soul and create intimacy with God that is not only believed but also experienced. You will discover both general and personal biblically based steps to find and nurture a genuinely immense connection with God, the lover of your soul!

Today, we live in the information age of expert panelists, sought-after public speakers, and experienced life coaches. All these, based on their credentials and experience, are viewed as qualified to speak on a particular topic. I am an inducted member of the International Society of Collegiate Scholars, formally educated in biblical studies at one of the largest universities in America. I was licensed and ordained into the ministry for over nineteen years. I have been a praise and worship leader for over twenty-two years, starting at a literal house church and eventually ending up at one of the biggest churches in the world, leading small groups to thousands of people into an intimate experience with God. But none of these credentials and experiences assisted in creating this book you hold in your hands right now. This book comes out of an intimate encounter with God in which God exposed how he feels in a way that I could feel and would never forget. This book will change your life forever.

I know the unsettling feeling of thinking that there has to be more. There has to be more than religious experiences typically experienced. There has to be more than the encounters that are manifested but are few and far between.

There has to be more to the feelings that I feel between the God that I believe exists. As human beings, we can express and experience love in ways that are felt. As human beings, we can invoke passionate feelings that can become destructive or constructive—and that is just between human beings. God not only expresses love but he is love. Which is the greater of the two? There has to be much more when it comes to our passionate connection with God. I am here to tell you that there is! Its theme flows through the entire Bible. It is so important to God that he inspired a complete book on the subject (Hosea), and God wants this connection so bad that he was willing to die for it. This book intends to help you to discover and fully develop the most profound, most passionate relationship with God that you have ever experienced. This book will change your life forever! If any part of this resonates within your being, let us settle these unsettling questions once and for all.

As the author of this book, I intend to guide as God breathes onto the pages of this book. There will be challenging moments for you to let go of your religious and theological practices and concepts that have stuck with you for years. I can attest to that. So here's the question: Is where you are currently producing the reality of God's word and a passionate connection? I am reminded of the great revelator apostle Paul's writing: "I count all things but loss for the excellency of the knowledge of Christ Jesus my Lord ... and do count them but dung, that I may win Christ ... Brethren, I count not myself to have apprehended: but this one thing I do, forgetting those things which are behind, and reaching forth unto those things which are before, I press toward the mark for the prize of the high calling of God in Christ Jesus" (Philippians 3:8, 13–14 KJV). If I secretly kept to myself all that is contained in these pages, I would fail God, myself, and all those who wrestle with the feeling that there has to be more.

My fellow seekers, my assignment is to lead you to the living water, but neither God nor I can make you drink. Are you ready? Are you ready to begin today? Are you eager to satisfy the deep longings of your heart when it comes to your God and Savior? Psalm 37:4 declares, "Delight thyself also in the Lord: and he shall give thee the desires of thine heart" (KJV). In other words, sometimes God puts desires and even unsettling feelings in our hearts to get us to pursue him and his kingdom. Are you ready? If so, let this book assist you in your pursuit.

Would you like to experience a new and miraculous relationship? Do you need a dramatic change in your life? Can you really have a connection with the Divine? If you desire a more fulfilling life, a heart transformation, and a soul lover who understands your every need, this book is right for you.

God, the Lover of Your Soul (Relationship, Not Religion) is a revolutionary book that opens your heart and mind to the power of God's unfathomable love. It removes the limitations of religion and exposes you to an intimate relationship with your Creator. Don't let religion kill your intimacy with God. Read on and experience true fulfillment. Will you trade your rituals and religious practices for an intimate, lasting relationship with Him? Discover a connection that is experienced and emotionally felt by God and You.

According to Genesis 1:26, "God said, Let us make man in our image, after our likeness" (KJV). If you have feelings of emotional needs and connections, where do you think you get them? You got them from God, who has similar feelings of emotional needs and connections. Humankind is also instructed to love God with all of one's mind and soul. Part of the soul houses the emotions, and God wants it all! Religion may appeal to our human nature, but it will not change our hearts. This book is all about a relationship that is emotionally felt between the eternal God and you! It is a connection that God wanted so immensely, he was willing to die for it.

In this book, there is a section at the end of each chapter for you to write down your reflections and notes on each chapter. Take your time read a chapter. Then ponder and meditate on what you read. Enjoy the journey of change and discovery!

—Hollis

Section One

The Truth about Love

chapter one

The Love of God

This book focuses on the phileo (or philia) version of love (the second most mention form of love in the Bible) and how it can fuel feelings and passions in your relationship with the creator. However, we must look at the agape form of love, the most foremost mentioned form of love in the Bible. Paul writes this scripture.

> And I pray that he would unveil within you the unlimited riches of his glory and favor until supernatural strength floods your innermost being with his divine might and explosive power. Then, by constantly using your faith, the life of Christ will be released deep inside you, and the resting place of his love will become the very source and root

of your life. Then you will be empowered to discover what every holy one experiences—the great magnitude of the astonishing love of Christ in all its dimensions. How deeply intimate and far-reaching is his love! How enduring and inclusive it is! Endless love beyond measurement that transcends our understanding—this extravagant love pours into you until you are filled to overflowing with the fullness of God! (Ephesians 3:16–19 TPT)

This particular passage of the Bible is taken from the Passion Translation Bible. Just a brief Bible study history note: The English language Bibles that we read are translated from handwritten documents from three other languages: Hebrew, Greek, and Aramaic. The Passion Translation Bible translates from the Aramaic language, which uses expressively passionate phrasing and words. In fact, you will notice this translation of Bible scriptures will be used throughout this book. That is intentional. After all, how can we approach a topic as God, the lover of our souls, without a translation that is expressively passionate? God's love is a passion that must be experienced and felt.

Ephesians 3:16–19 was Paul's prayer for the believers in Ephesus. His heartfelt desire was that they, as well as all believers, would come to experience the love that he had— the kind of love that only comes from the Creator himself. Our human attempts to try to describe that kind of love fall short. "Agape is the highest of the four types of love in the Bible. This term defines God's immeasurable, incomparable love for humankind. It is the divine love that comes from God. Agape love is perfect, unconditional, sacrificial, and pure."[1] Even with the scriptural and English definition, this form of love will ever be indescribable. It must be experienced and felt. To receive love from someone who is capable of loving you is one of the greatest experiences to have in this life; think of the love of a parent, a family member, a friend, or a lover. But to receive deep love from someone who is not only capable but whose whole being is love is something altogether different. Scripture declares that God is love, and 1 John 4:8 declares, "He that loveth not knoweth not God; for God is love" (KJV).

The love that flows from him is more intense than any love you have ever felt in your life. It is more significant than the feeling you felt for a boyfriend or girlfriend. It is higher than the feeling you felt from your parents. It is greater than the feeling that is felt from a spouse or a

---

[1] "Explore 4 Different Types of Love in the Bible," Learn Religions

child. This love is what Paul was trying to explain and pray for concerning the Ephesians. But here is the issue: most people, whether believers or nonbelievers, do not believe that is even possible. "How am I able to connect with someone who is so esteemed and powerful, and whose entire being glows with the deepest love I have ever experienced and longed for?" This book seeks to provide a compass, a GPS, a blueprint for just that answer. But you must at least open up your mind to the possibility of such an experience. Attempt to take off religion and replace it with a relationship that is not only understood but also experienced. There is much to say about the love of God, but his desire is that you experience it in reality, so you have something to say about his love yourself. Remember, phileo is the fuel for all types of love moving a person to passionately respond and experience love in correct, loving ways.

Chapter Reflections and Notes

chapter two

The Intensity of God's Love for Us

God's intense interest in us is something that most of us never think about. The Creator of the massively expanding universe with all its stars, planets, and galaxies. The Creator who created our sun, which can fit over a million globes of Earths in it. The Creator of all plants, animals, and humanity. This same Creator, the God of heaven and Earth, wants us and is so deeply interested in us with detail in a way that no one else will ever be. He is so interested in us that he has not just counted each hair on our head but has them numbered.

The average human head has about one hundred thousand hairs with a similar number of hair follicles. When a single strand of hair falls out, he notices it as hair number 72,345. The disciple Luke declares,

> Are not five sparrows sold for two copper
> coins? Yet not one of them has [ever] been
> forgotten in the presence of God. Indeed, the
> very hairs of your head are all numbered. Do
> not be afraid; you are far more valuable than
> many sparrows. (Luke 12:6–7 AMP)

We all have deep needs as individuals. I would assume not one of us longs to have our hairs counted or numbered. It is a tremendous benefit and privilege to have someone so powerful and perfectly loving be interested in you in that way.

Only God, the lover of our souls, could endure such a sacrificial amount of pain and still desire to passionately connect with us in such a way. The writing of John passionately declares,

> God did not send his Son into the world
> to judge and condemn the world, but to be
> its Savior and rescue it! So now there is no
> longer any condemnation for those who
> believe in him, but the unbeliever already
> lives under condemnation because they do
> not believe in the name of God's beloved
> son. (John 3:17–18 TPT)

Religion says God sent Jesus to die so that you would not have to be condemned to hell. But relationship says God's passion to be intimately connected with you is so intense that he was willing to die for the opportunity to be the lover of your soul. Once this loving connected felt relationship is established, there is nothing external that can disconnect us from his love.

> For I am persuaded that neither death nor life, nor angels nor principalities nor powers, nor things present nor things to come, nor height nor depth, nor any other created thing, shall be able to separate us from the love of God which is in Christ Jesus our Lord. (Romans 8:38–39 NKJV)

God has been in pursuit of us since before the fall of Adam and Eve in the garden. Revelation 13:8 states, "… whose names have not been written in the Book of Life of the Lamb slain from the foundation of the world" (NKJV). It may be true that Jesus Christ did not have a human body until the immaculate conception of Mary. This scripture is implying that the solution needed to reconcile fallen man back to God was created before it was needed. This pre-created plan is an expression to God's all-knowing ability and his passionate, pursuing love for us. Isaiah 46:9–10 declares, "Remember the former things of old: for I am God, and there is none else; I am God, and there is none like me, Declaring the end from the beginning, and from ancient times the things that are not yet done" (NKJV). You have never had, nor will you ever have, anybody want you this badly. God never wants us to experience the results of our bad decisions and actions while having to respect our free will. But he is driven by his love, and he provides solutions in advance, even if it may cost his life.

The feelings and needs that we have include being loved, words of affirmation, being appreciated, receiving gifts, affection, acts of love, respect, and quality time. Where do you think they came from? Genesis 1:26–27 records,

> Then God said, "Let Us [Father, Son, Holy Spirit] make man in Our image, according to Our likeness [not physical, but a spiritual personality and moral likeness]; and let them have complete authority over the fish of the sea, the birds of the air, the cattle, and over the entire earth, and over everything that creeps *and* crawls on the earth." So, God created man in His own image, in the image *and* likeness of God He created him. (AMP)

We are created in the image and likeness of God. Therefore, we have some of his traits. In other words, those feelings and needs just listed came from God. He has the ability to identify with us through those feelings. Hebrews 4:15 declares, "For we have not a high priest which cannot be touched with the FEELING of our infirmities" (KJV). Ephesians 4:30 records, "And grieve not the holy Spirit of God, whereby ye are sealed unto the day of redemption" (KJV). Grief is a deep form of sadness. So not only does the lover of your soul has feelings, but his feelings are intense.

Those feelings and needs are satisfied through intimate connection with creation (humanity) and through the true worship that is expressed from humanity. To worship means "To adore; to pay divine honors to; to reverence with supreme respect and veneration [dedication]."[2] The desire to be worshiped and adored is entirely reserved for God. No other being, human or otherwise, is to be worshiped. John 4:23–24 declares, "But the hour is coming, and now is, when the true worshipers will worship the Father in spirit and truth; for the Father is seeking such to worship Him. God is Spirit, and those who worship Him must worship in spirit and truth" (NKJV). The word *seeking* in this scripture describes a version of desire that has moved into active pursuit mode. *Webster's Dictionary*

---

[2] Webster, N. (2015).

of 1828 defines the verb *seek* as to go after, to search or quest for, to search for by going from place to place.[3] The need of God to be worshiped and adored is so strong that it has moved him from the desired state to actively pursuing the satisfaction of that need. Being the omniscient, all-knowing God, he had to have known that there would be some in his creation who would never love him in that way. But that does not remove the fact that those needs are real true feelings and needs. You know how you act when you get what you want and need. Can you imagine how the Creator will act after obtaining the satisfying intimacy and worship he desires so much from us? His desire is so strong that he was willing to die for it, letting his creation betray him, spit in his face, whip him till his guts hang out, and crucify him to restore the possibility of obtaining his need—and not the guarantee of receiving the love and worship, but just the chance.

---

[3] Webster, N. (2015).

Chapter Reflections and Notes

_____

_____

_____

_____

_____

_____

_____

_____

_____

_____

_____

_____

_____

_____

_____

_____

chapter three

The Secrets of the Suffering Savior

There are some factors and benefits that have been accomplished through the suffering of the Savior of this world, Jesus Christ (Yeshua). Those sufferings have been depicted in the Bible, and in the visual arts through movies and paintings. It appears that we have benefited more from the Savior's suffering than the Savior himself, and it is through his sufferings that all humanity has obtained certain benefits that we may not be fully aware of.

2nd Corinthians 8:9 says,

> For you have experienced the extravagant grace of our Lord Jesus Christ, that although he was infinitely rich, he impoverished himself for our sake, so that by his poverty,

we could become rich [abundantly blessed] beyond measure. (TPT)

The blessing is inclusive of every area of our lives: financially, physically, socially, emotionally, mentally, and spiritually. As I was meditating on the Savior's sufferings, I discovered significant benefits that have revolutionized the way I view his sufferings and my level of appreciation. These benefits are the benefits of the soul and mind and freedom from excessive hard work.

If you ever have seen the movie *The Passion of the Christ*, you were given an adequate visual depiction of the extreme physical torture that Jesus (Yeshua) endured. If you have never seen this movie, I suggest that you do so. This movie is a graphic, horrific, and barbaric illustration of Jesus (God wrapped in human flesh), allowing himself to be subjected to such a horrible experience. This is the equivalent of parents experiencing their child bringing false accusations and false witnesses against them. It's like allowing themselves to be physically assaulted in court, while the child spits in their faces. Then a bag is put on their heads while they are punched and mocked, with the accusers saying, "Tell us who hit you in the face!" But it did not stop there. Jesus was then handed over to the Roman Empire to be whipped at the whipping post till his internal organs were exposed. Then later he was hung on wooden posts by his hands and feet, then pierced in his side with a spear. Crucifixion was a torturous, graphic death.

Translate this horrible, graphic physical experience to the mental state of the soul experiencing something similar, not physically but mentally. Just like his physical body was made a sacrifice for our benefit, so was his soul and mind made a sacrifice for our benefit. In the story of Jesus in the Garden of Gethsemane, he said something very interesting.

> Then Jesus came with them to a place called Gethsemane, and said to the disciples, "Sit here while I go and pray over there." And He took with Him Peter and the two sons of Zebedee, and He began to be sorrowful and deeply distressed. Then He said to them, "My soul is exceedingly sorrowful, even to death. Stay here and watch with Me." (Matthew 26:36–38 NKJV)

What could have bothered the Savior of the world that much? He was not just sad but sorrowful, and sorrow is sadness on steroids. And he was not just sorrowful but exceedingly sorrowful. What on earth could inflict that much emotional distress on the God of heaven and earth?

Isaiah, the eagle-eyed prophet, gives us a glimpse of the answer when he declared,

> Yet it pleased the Lord [was his solution] to bruise him; he hath put him to grief: when thou shalt make his soul an offering for sin... (Isaiah 53:10 KJV)

So not only was his body made a sacrifice for all humanity, but his soul was simultaneously made a sacrifice. While his body was brutally ravaged, he had every soulish and mental issue there would ever be placed on him all at once. These mental issues include fear, anxiety, Alzheimer's, schizophrenia, worry, overwhelming sorrow, PTSD, Autism, and any other soul or mental disorder. Most people get medical help and a prescription after suffering from just one of these disorders. Yet Jesus, with his amazing love for us, endured all this at once in order for us to not have to experience such things.

Another form of his sufferings was the crowns of thorns, which was placed on his head. This suffering was also to benefit us. The type of thorns used to ridicule him as king was made of thorns, which were more like surgical needles. After being lied on, betrayed, wrongly convicted, spit on, beaten with a bag on his head (while demanding that he prophesy and tell who hit him in his face), and whipped until his organs were hanging out, they placed this skin-piercing crown of thorns on his head. The powerful thing that benefited us is the moment the first thorn pierced his skin and touched his blood; it removed the curse of old. The blood of the New Covenant made contact with the crown thorns on his head and the cursed of thorns in the garden found in the book of Genesis. "Adam, the ground is cursed because of you. All your life you will struggle to scratch a living from it. It will grow thorns and thistles for you" (Genesis 3:17–18 NLT). The crown of thorns was used to remove the curse of thorns and excessive hard work by the power of his blood. All praise and worship to the lover of our souls now and forever!

Chapter Reflections and Notes

chapter four

The Tabernacle: The Blueprint for Divine Intimacy

The wilderness tabernacle gives us clues concerning God's dislikes and likes. These clues are significant. It would be very disappointing to be in a relationship with someone who does not even have a clue about your likes and dislikes, even more so if that relationship has accumulated over a certain amount of time. God never liked the system of sacrifice he gave in the wilderness to the people of Israel. The sacrifice was never pleasing to him. It never gave him satisfying pleasure. He even says it in his Word: "Therefore, when He [Jesus] came into the world, He said: 'Sacrifice and offering You did not desire, But a body You have prepared for Me. In burnt offerings and *sacrifices* for sin. You had no pleasure'" (Hebrews 10:5–7 NKJV). The sacrifice of bulls and goats in the wilderness tabernacle was a temporary fix for the spiritual adultery of sin. It was sort of like putting a bandage on a wound until the healing took place. That healing would be in the form of Jesus (Yeshua). But even that sacrifice was nothing God liked, or that was pleasurable to him.

Before you begin to conjure up scripture references in your mind to dispute this statement, let us examine a familiar scripture, Isaiah 53:10. "Yet it pleased the Lord to bruise him; he hath put him to grief: when thou shalt make his soul an offering for sin, he shall see his seed" (KJV). At first it would seem this text disproves the previous statement, and that God liked and got the pleasure of the horrific torture of his only begotten son. There is a biblical study tool that is called textual criticism. It does not mean to criticize the text of the Bible. What it means is to use several different translations of scripture to gather a more informed meaning of the text. Let's look at that same scripture in the Amplified translation. "Yet the Lord was willing To crush Him, causing Him to suffer; If He would give Himself as a guilt offering [an atonement for sin], He shall see *His* [spiritual] offspring" (Isaiah 53:10 AMP). The sacrifices where never anything pleasurable to God, but they were his will (intention) and means to get to the source of his real desire and pleasure: us. Jesus further clarifies this in the Garden:

He asked the father: "Going a little farther, he fell with his face to the ground and prayed,..."O My Father, if it is possible, let this cup pass from Me; nevertheless, not as I will, but as You *will*." (Matthew 26:39 NKJV)

While hanging on the cross Jesus [Yeshua] later asked the Father "My God, My God, why have You forsaken Me? (Matthew 27:46 NKJV)

God the Father neither liked nor experienced anything pleasurable at that moment. There is nothing pleasurable or to be desired in both horrific moments of sacrifice. That is why both sacrifices took place on the outside. Jesus's sacrifice took place outside the city, and the sacrifices of bulls and goats were in the outer court of the tabernacle, away from where the pillar of fire of the Arc of the Covenant was, in the tabernacle.

Much like sacrifices, praise is another outer court experience. Psalm 100:4 says, "Enter into his gates with thanksgiving, and into his courts with praise" (KJV). Praise and ceremonial sacrifices are viewed as biblical requirements. But neither guaranteed a pleasurable experience that God would like. Anyone breathing can praise him and then walk away because of no intimate connection. Some only praise him because they want something from him, yet they do not want him. There is a familiar scripture in the Bible that most believers can quote, found in John 4:23. "But the hour is coming, and now is, when the true worshippers shall worship the Father in spirit and in truth: for the Father is seeking such to worship him" (NKJV). God not seeking praise indicates that praise does not entirely satisfy him. Think about that: God, who knows all, who created all, and by whom all things exist, is seeking something else. Whatever that something is has to be extremely important. To seek something means to move from desire to active pursuit of something, further putting a strong emphasis on what he likes, the one thing that really brings him pleasure. You know how you act when you get something you really want? Can you imagine how God will act when we give him what he wants?

The gates, the courts, the sacrifices, and the praises are all experiences that were designed to lead us and give us the ability to go into secret places where the lover of our souls awaits. Now let us transition from the outside (the outer experiences) to the area of intimacy (the Holy of Holies). It is in deep, intimate areas that one discovers the likes and dislikes of our creator. The veil of the tabernacle and the temple are much like the bedroom doors of a husband and wife. This area is the relationship God often uses as an example of our relationship with him. Just as with a husband and wife, it is in the private area of the bedroom that intimacy and pleasures are exchanged. In the same manner, it was behind the veil that the exchange of intimacy and worship would take place. It is also in this intimate place that God gives us a glimpse of his intention to save us. If you took an aerial view of the layout behind the veil, it would take on the shape of a cross. The area on the wooden cross where Jesus would hang his head and die would have lined up with the same area of the Holy Place in the tabernacle.

Chapter Reflections and Notes

_____

_____

_____

_____

_____

_____

_____

_____

_____

_____

_____

_____

_____

_____

_____

_____

chapter five

The Prophet Hosea and the Erasing of the God Factor

The following story illustrates the painful actions of an unfaithful lover and the responses of the one who has been hurt and offended. Imagine a faithful husband who has been trying to please and take care of his wife but often catches her repeatedly in bed with one of her lovers. The unfaithful lover says,

> I will go after my lovers [more than one], who give me my food and my water, my wool and my linen, my olive oil and my drink [her needs]." The husband, "she decked herself with her earrings and her jewels, and she went after her lovers, and forgot me" [me? How could she forget about me?]. "I gave

her corn [food], and wine, and oil, and multiplied her silver and gold" [I gave her what she wanted and needed, and she forgets about me?]. (Hosea 2:5, 13, 8 NIV)

The offended husband's response:

Let her put away her harlotries from her sight. And her adulteries from between her breasts; Lest I strip her naked. And expose her, as in the day she was born, And make her like a wilderness, And set her like a dry land, And slay her with thirst. "I will not have mercy on her children, For they *are* the children of harlotry. For their mother has played the harlot; She who conceived them has behaved shamefully [The reaction to such a hurtful situation!]. (Hosea 2:2–5 NKJV)

Before you become judgmental of the reaction, put yourself on the painful side of the story. What if you were the one who has been giving of yourself for the selfless satisfaction of your significant other, and your significant other has to want for nothing physically, emotionally, or financially? You happen to come home early one day to be treated to an unforgettable visual of your significant other intimately intertwined in the bed with a lover, and this is only the first of multiple times. You can imagine the level of pain. How would you feel? Think about it for a moment. Get past all the anger and ask yourself, "How would I feel?" The reaction in the story is all the language of a painful response. This story is ripped right off of the pages of the Bible, from the book of Hosea. The book of Hosea is one of the attempts of God to get us to understand he has feelings too, and how we make him feel at times.

In fact, it is so important to him that he created an entire book on this matter, the book of the prophet Hosea. God specifically chose the relationship between a husband and wife as a reference point so that we could have a clear understanding. He has done so in hopes that we all individually have an "aha" epiphany moment. We recognize that he has feelings too, and every time we do something wrong, it is the equivalent to catching your lover in bed with another. Every time we sin or turn to gods that don't even exist, we inflict this pain upon him again and again. When we sin, it is not just about doing wrong, God's judgment, or God's punishment. It is more so about the separating pain that is inflicted upon God and ultimately upon us. Ephesians 4:30 pleads with us, "Grieve not the holy Spirit of God, whereby ye are sealed unto the day of redemption" (KJV). We cause him grief on a level from which most would not hesitate to distance themselves. But it goes even deeper than that. Take that emotional pain that you imagine from this story and multiply it by the over seven billion people who populate the earth now. That is the pain God is feeling.

For generations upon generations, the Heavenly Father (God) has been using the relationship of a husband and wife as an example of our relationship with him. Isaiah 54:5 reads, "For your Maker (the one who made us) is your husband, the Lord of Hosts is His name; and your Redeemer is the Holy One of Israel; He shall be called the God of the whole earth" (KJV). Ephesians 5:25 states, "Husbands love your wives, even as Christ also loved the church, and gave himself for it" (KJV). One of the driving forces of the modern-day culture is to dilute, confuse, and generationally remove the biblical example of a husband and wife relationship. This removal will affectively remove the point of reference to how we are to relate to our God and maker. These actions will eventually lead to the removal of God himself out of the conscious mind, and then ultimately forgetting about even his existence.

The global move to remove Yahweh, the God of the Bible, from society is the equivalent of being in a room full of people, and someone who knows you greets everyone but completely ignores you. Imagine the offense and the disrespect. Today, we are living in an environment of systematic attempts to remove the consciousness of God's existence out of our minds, cultures, and daily lives. The result would be the removal of God, the lover of your soul, in the hope that you would turn to other lovers. Those lovers may seek control of the way you think, your beliefs, and ultimately you.

One of those systematic attempts is evolution. It is everywhere. It is in museums. It is in grade-school classrooms. It is in the lecture halls of prestigious universities. I had the privilege of studying the evolution of evolution. The most well-known modern icon of evolution is Charles Darwin (1809–1882). Though his concept of evolution is widely used and accepted, he was not the first. There was Aristotle (394–322 BC) with his concept of "Scala Nature," which ranked living and nonliving things on a ladder. Then there was Jean Baptiste Lamark (1744–1829). Then there are the two Sir Charles Darwin piggybacked off of, Charles Lyell with *Principles of Geology* and Thomas Malthus with *An Essay on the Principle of Population*.[4] One of the shocking and not commonly known discoveries about Sir Charles Darwin was that he obtained a degree in theology. Theology is "the science (the systematic study)

---

[4] Dewitt, Ph.D., D. A. (2012).

of God and divine things; or the science which teaches the existence, character and attributes of God."[5] Later, Sir Charles Darwin would have his teachings from his book, *On the Origin of Species*, to be modernized and widely used to erase the existence of God the creator. Also, in this same book Sir Charles makes a contradicting statement on evolution:

> To supposed that the eye, with all of its inimitable contrivances for adjusting focus to different distances, for admitting different amounts of light, and for the correction of spherical and chromatic aberration, could have been informed by natural selection, seems, I freely confess, absurd in the highest possible degree.[6]

Yet the common thought of today is that we evolved from some chimpanzee, gorilla, or monkey. Google images of the legendary Big Foot. Now, are you willing to take him to your next family reunion and inform your family this is their long-lost, distant relative? What do you think the response will be? If we are descendants of monkeys, what evidence do we have? We can find criminals and fugitives

---

[5] Webster, N. (2015).
[6] Darwin, C. (2003).

who have vehicles, weapons, passports, and assistance. But we have yet to find Big Foot for generations.

Let's look at the fossil records. Maybe we could trace our ancestors back to apes. First up, the Piltdown skull proved to be a hoax of a partial human jaw and ape skull pieced together. Next is "Lucy" (Australopithecus), the supposed primate fossil remains of our ancestral link. Lucy's fossil remains, which were only 40 percent with only fragmented small pieces of a skull and hip, were scattered bones with no hands and feet that were pieced together.[7] The characteristics of the skull and hip have distinguishing differences between apes and us. Yet Lucy is presented in most museums today as a female primate with human characteristics made from a full man-made cast image (with full skull and hips), and museums do not inform us of this. Now, let us try the possibility of DNA technology to connect to apes being our missing evolutionary link. DNA technology is the same technology used to convict criminals and free wrongly convicted prisoners of crimes. It turns out we have key DNA differences as it relates to apes. [8] Humans have twenty-three chromosomes and

---

[7] Dewitt, Ph.D., D. A. (2012).

[8] Dewitt, Ph.D., D. A. (2012).

chimps have twenty-four. Human telomeres are half as long.[9]

All this falsehood represents the tactics used by the enemy of our souls since creation to get us to forget who God is and who we are. If you do not know who you are, you are bound to be controlled by those who do. Lucifer (Satan) first got Adam and Eve to lose consciousness of who they really were. Genesis 3:4–5 records, "The serpent said to the woman, 'You certainly will not die! For God knows that on the day you eat from it your eyes will be opened [that is, you will have greater awareness], and you will be like God'" (AMP). Excuse me, Adam and Eve. You were already like God. That was a crafty play on words by Satan. Genesis 1:27 states, "So God created man (humans) in His own image, in the image and likeness of God He created him; male and female He created them" (AMP). Remember, dear reader, your divine value and divine worth. Ignore anything or anyone that tries to diminish it, such attempts are not coming from the Creator, the lover of your soul. "I will give thanks and praise to You, for I am fearfully and wonderfully made; Wonderful are Your works, And my soul knows it very well" (Psalm 139:14 AMP).

---

[9] Dewitt, Ph.D., D. A. (2012).

Chapter Reflections and Notes

chapter six

The Four Types of Love and the Feeling Factor of the Heart, Soul, and Mind

This chapter maybe the one demanding chapter in this book for some. Due to the technical definitions of the types of love described. But, this is a necessary journey in order to experience the type of love this book is centered around, Phileo. The type of love that is connective and emotionally felt. Do not be derailed the rest of the book gets much easier. So, read on! There are four types of love mentioned in the Bible, derived from four Greek words: *agape, eros, storge,* and *philia* (or *phileo*). Agape (pronounced uh-GAH-pay) is the highest of the four types of love in the Bible. Agape defines God's unbound, unequaled love for humankind.[10]

---

[10] "Explore 4 Different Types of Love in the Bible," Learn Religions

Eros (pronounced AIR-ohs) is the Greek word for sensual or romantic love. The term describes physical love, sexual desire, physical attraction, and physical affection—love expressed through physical means.[11] Storge (pronounced STOR-jay) is a word for love in the Bible that may be unfamiliar. This Greek word describes familiar love. It is the love of affectionate bonds that develops naturally between parents and children, siblings, and the extended family.[12] Philia or phileo (pronounced FILL-ee-o) is the type of intimate love in the Bible that most Christians practice toward one another. But the possibility of such a form of love is rarely talked about as an experience between humanity and God. This Greek term describes powerful, mutually deep emotional bonds.[13] Philia or phileo is the second most mentioned type of love in the Bible after agape.

There are two other diverted forms of love not found in the Bible passed down through time, *ludus* and *pragma*. These two possible types of love are self-centered. Perhaps that clarifies why they are not mentioned in the Bible.

The Bible describes love in this manner:

---

[11] "Explore 4 Different Types of Love in the Bible," Learn Religions
[12] "Explore 4 Different Types of Love in the Bible," Learn Religions
[13] "Explore 4 Different Types of Love in the Bible," Learn Religions

Love is large and incredibly patient. Love is gentle and consistently kind to all. It refuses to be jealous when blessing comes to someone else. Love does not brag about one's achievements nor inflate its own importance. Love does not traffic in shame and disrespect, nor selfishly seek its own honor. Love is not easily irritated or quick to take offense. Love joyfully celebrates honesty and finds no delight in what is wrong. Love is a safe place of shelter, for it never stops believing the best for others. Love never takes failure as defeat, for it never gives up. Love never stops loving. (1 Corinthians 13:4–8 TPT)

For this book, *God, the Lover of Your Soul,* the focus will be on the form of love called phileo. Phileo is the type of passionate, intimate love in the Bible that some believers practice only toward one another. Phileo is the driving force for all types of love, moving a person to respond in heartfelt, correct loving ways. Philia originates from the Greek term *phíleo* meaning, "someone dearly loved [prized] in a personal, intimate way; a trusted confidant held dear in a close bond of personal affection." Philia expresses an experience-based love.[14] What if the philia form of love with all its affection and feelings was used and experienced in relationship with God, the lover of your soul? This would be part of the fulfillment of the greatest commandment. In the Bible, you are instructed to love God with all your soul. Your soul contains your emotions and feelings, and God wants all of it.

The phileo version of love is the type of love that deals with feelings and passions. The verb *phileo* means "to have ardent affection and feeling."[15] It is also described as fondness and personal attachment. It represents a variety of intensely close emotional bonds. Phileo love is essential, and it must be valuable to God, the lover of your soul. This can be intimidating if you are not a person who is in touch with or used to dealing with your feelings in a meaningful, beneficial way. Don't be intimidated; every one of us, as God's creations, comes with the ability to feel love in an emotional, affectionate way. God would never require something of us that could not be done. That would make him unjust or unfair. It must be discovered or rediscovered. Also, you must not wait till you feel it to do it; you must do it till you feel it.

One follower of Christ, Mark, records a fascinating conversation Jesus had with the religious leaders of that day. The Bible records

> Then one of the scribes came, and having heard them reasoning together, perceiving that He had answered them well, asked Him, "Which is the first commandment of all?" Jesus answered him, "The first of all the commandments is ... the Lord is one. And you shall love the Lord your God with all your heart, with all your soul, with all your mind, and with all your strength. This is the first commandment. And the second, like it, is this: You shall love your neighbor as yourself. There is no other commandment greater than these." (Mark 12:28–31 NKJV)

The heart is mentioned over eight hundred times in scripture but never referring to the physical pump that drives blood. The original Greek word that was translated to our English language is *kardia*. Kardía (the heart) is best defined as "the affective center of our being," the capacity of moral preference (volitional desire, choice), the "desire-producer that makes us tick", or our "desire-decisions" that establish who we really are. Some say it is your spirit.[16]

The soul (Greek: *psuché*) is described as the place of our affections and desires. This word occurs over one hundred times in the Bible. The soul and its capabilities are the direct result of God breathing (blowing) his gift of life into the first person, making him an ensouled being, as in Genesis 2:7 (KJV), which says, "And the Lord God formed man of the dust of the ground, and breathed into his nostrils the breath of life; and man became a living soul." The soul and its characteristics are what separate us from other creatures and human-made creations (i.e., artificial intelligence).[17] The origin of the soul also amplifies the importance of its capabilities of affection and desire. From his mouth, God spoke the universe and all creation into existence. He then turns around with his same mouth and breathes the breath of life including the soul with all its affections and passion into humans.

The mind. The original Greek word in this scripture is *diánoia*, literally meaning "thorough reasoning," which

---

[16] "Strong's Greek: 2588. καρδία (kardia) – Heart."

[17] "Strong's Greek: 5590. ψυχή (psuché) -- Breath, the Soul."

incorporates both sides of a matter to reach a meaningful conclusion.[18]

After discovering the form of love called phileo and the ability to connect with God in this way, our understanding of scripture is dramatically changed for the better. Three scriptures come to mind. The first is the greatest commandment: "Love the Lord your God with every passion of your heart, with all the energy of your being, and with every thought that is within you. This is the great and supreme commandment" (Matthew 22:37–38 TPT). This scripture now moves away from a religious command to a natural response. Another familiar scripture is John 14:15 (NKJV), which says, "If you love Me, keep My commandments. "This scripture also moves from a command to a natural response. It is now translated to, "Loving me empowers you to obey my commands" (John 14:15 TPT). Then there is this familiar scripture:

> For this is how much God loved the world
> (his human creation) he gave his one and
> only, unique Son as a gift. So now everyone
> who believes in him will never perish but
> experience everlasting life. God did not send

---

[18] "Strong's Greek: 1271. διάνοια (dianoia) -- The Mind, Disposition, Thought."

his Son into the world to judge and condemn
the world, but to be its Savior and rescue it!
(John 3:16-17 TPT)

To rescue someone from an impending danger requires
a certain amount of passionate concern. Phileo is the same
type of feeling that will drive someone into a burning
building to save his or her loved one. Phileo is the type
of love that God the Creator has for us. Salvation is not
just about you making it into heaven or being saved from
wrath and eternal damnation. It is more so about God's
strong, passionate desire to connect with us, his human
creation—whom he was willing to die for to restore the
connection with.

Emotions have frequencies. Every emotional reaction
or stimulation produces a frequency. Love is a frequency,
and so is hate. When you are in a situation where there is
a lot of anger, tension, and hatred, you can feel it. That is
because emotions have a spectacular ability to transmit
frequencies that can change the atmosphere of a room.
Have you ever walked into a room where the conflict was
so intense that you could feel it? Some people even say,
"I could cut the tension in the atmosphere with a knife."
Have you ever felt your spouse upset with you without him
or her saying a word? Why is that? It is because emotions

can produce feelings that can be felt and experienced. The more connected the relationship, the easier and stronger the emotion is felt and transmitted, even to the degree that a couple, based on their level of connection, can simultaneously have the same thought or feeling before either one communicates it. The same with us and God (the lover of our souls). Just as aggression and danger can emit frequencies altering an atmosphere and experiences, so can love. The type of love that deals with feeling is so important. It is called phileo, and it is the second most mentioned version of love in the Bible after agape, the supreme love, for a reason. Where is it, and how is it experienced? It is transmitted in your brain—the collection of tissue in your head that works by electrical frequencies. Go figure. Located in the temporal lobe, emotions like love are carried out by the limbic system. The center of emotional processing is the amygdala, which receives input from other brain functions. According to Shippensburg University, this almond-shaped tissue is responsible for multiple emotional responses, like love and sexual desire. The hippocampus sends information to the amygdala based on emotional ties. According to the Canadian Institutes of Health Research, the prefrontal cortex is involved in decision making in response to emotions. The hypothalamus acts as a regulator of emotions and pleasure by controlling their levels. The ventral tegmental area is also involved in how a person perceives pleasure.[19] Because these are the areas from which the feelings of love are processed, it would make sense of the creator's request for us to love him with all our minds and souls. As recorded in Matthew 22:36–38, "Master, which is the great commandment in the law? Jesus said unto him, Thou shalt love the Lord thy God with all thy heart, and with all thy soul, and with all thy mind" (KJV). Your emotions are located in your soul, and he wants all of it. God requires us to love him from the core of who we are with emotion and affection, not void of any intellectual reasoning, and to do it to the fullest.

---

[19] Stannard, L. "What Parts of the Human Brain Correspond to Emotion or Love?"

Chapter Reflections and Notes

_____

_____

_____

_____

_____

_____

_____

_____

_____

_____

_____

_____

_____

_____

_____

_____

Section Two

The Interferences to Intimacy with God

chapter seven

The Imagery and Language
of Slaves and Servants

Christians believe that God loves them as his children. However, some believe that he will punish them whenever they commit any evil, though 90 percent believe that this is not a withdrawal of God's love. Other Christians believe that at this point, God's love has reduced.[20] Nonetheless, Christian's love for God varies. For some, this depends on the circumstances they are facing at the moment. Some believe that God may have left them to struggle with their problems that cannot be avoided in this life. This may subconsciously cause some believers to not have a strong love for him (God). Similarly, 97 percent of nonbelievers do not have any association with God and hence can never

---

[20] Underhill, E. (2015).

commit to love him in any way.[21] With such murky imagery of God's love toward us, the passionate drive to pursue him and his love would be nonenergetic and religious at best.

This distorted image of the Creator is so pervasive in the minds of this modern world that we even have an insurance disaster clause called "an act of God." Think about it: if your view of God has shaped him as a heartless taskmaster and the executor of judgment, would you think of passionately pursuing him? Similarly, if you believe that we are left to fend for ourselves in a world that will be filled with constant hardship and grief, and there is an Almighty God who cannot do anything about that, why are you as a believer praising a powerless God? Why would Jesus (Yeshua) come here endure all he endured on the cross, only for you to go through the same hardship you would have experienced had he just stayed in heaven? The probability of you passionately pursuing him and experience an intimate loving relationship with him is not going to be felt. The heavenly Father sums up this distorted view with this statement: "'For I know the plans and thoughts that I have for you,' says the Lord, 'plans for peace and well-being and not for disaster, to give you a future and a hope'" (Jeremiah 29:11 AMP). In other words, don't tell him his plans and thoughts toward you. Let him tell

---

[21] Underhill, E. (2015).

you his heart toward you. Your imagery may be distorted. Jesus (Yeshua) comes later in the New Testament to back up the words of the heavenly Father with this statement: "The thief cometh not, but for to steal, and to kill, and to destroy: I am come that they might have life, and that they might have it more abundantly" (John 10:10 KJV). Anyone or anything that comes to steal, kill, or destroy any area of our lives is not coming from them. In order to start growing in experiencing intimacy with your creator (God The Lover of Your Soul) a mind change in the way we view him must take place. But it is not only a mind change in the way we view him. It also requires a 180-degree shift in the way we view our relationship position and the language we use in the relationship. The Word of God records in Romans,

> For all who are allowing themselves to be led
> by the Spirit of God are sons of God. For you
> have not received a spirit of *slavery* leading
> again to fear [of God's judgment], but you
> have received the Spirit of adoption as sons
> [the Spirit producing sonship] by which we
> [joyfully] cry, "Abba! Father!" The Spirit
> Himself testifies and confirms together with

our spirit [assuring us] that we [believers] are children of God. (Romans 8:14–16 AMP)

Jesus then tells us,

You show that you are my intimate friends … I have never called you 'servants,' because a master doesn't confide in his **servants**, and servants don't always understand what the master is doing. But I call you my most intimate friends, for I reveal to you everything that I've heard from my Father. (John 15:14–15 TPT)

With this understanding, words like *serve* and *obey* become recognized words of slaves and servants, which should be changed to words like *satisfy* and *passionately desire to do*. Masters and slave owners do not die for their slaves and servants. Masters or slave owners typically have no desire to have a beneficial intimate relationship with their slaves and servants.

Chapter Reflections and Notes

chapter eight

The Mind versus Religion

Religion has tried to cover the festering sores of the soul with practical solutions, entertainment, and things that may make you feel good but only for the moment. If these religious solutions were so affective, why has humanity grown exceedingly worse over time? The answer has always been and will always be spiritual, and that spirituality is an intimate connection with the one and only true living God. Religion requires you to stop the use of your brain's ability to think. It requires you to worship in the temple at the altar of foolishness. Relationship includes the use of your intellectual mind. It is part of the greatest commandment in the Bible. Religion says that there has to be more than one God (the supreme being). The mind says that that doesn't make sense because if there is more than one God (the supreme being), he ceases to be supreme. After all, there would be others just like him. Religion requires the worship of created deities in the form of trees, plants, monkeys, rats, and the like. The mind says that it does not make sense, because how is God going to help me when I can create an axe, pesticides, a gun, and rat poison to kill him? Religion says I can use a creation of God such as a crystal carving for protection. The mind says that this does not make sense when I can make a quick trip to the local hardware store to purchase a sledgehammer, then use this hammer to destroy the very object that was supposed to protect me. Religion says that there are many ways to God. The mind says that is like playing spiritual roulette and gambling with the possibility of a tragic end. What if I am wrong? Religion says God is a force of the evolving universe. The mind says it is impossible to be intimate with the universe. All these concepts are why I so dislike religion, despite being licensed and ordained for over nineteen years.

It is very important to be clear and focused on the object of your intimate spiritual connection. This is as vital in our relationship with God even as it is in our natural relationships with humanity (i.e., your spouse, children, your parents). Those of us who are professed believers in the Judeo-Christian faith are not immune to the subtle seduction of religion. Religion would have us to fall in love with the practices and systems of God, simultaneously not realizing the disconnection with the God of the practices and systems. Religion says when praises go up, blessings come down! Imagine how insulting it must be to God—to offer God some adoration or praise in hope that it satisfies him enough to release some type a blessing or benefit is a contaminated form of praise, as if God has no idea your other motives for praising him. "All the ways of a man are clean *and* innocent in his own eyes [and he may see nothing wrong with his actions], But the Lord weighs *and* examines the motives *and* intents [of the heart and knows the truth]" (Proverbs 16:2 AMP). Praise to God must be strictly for him and unto him; nothing more, nothing less.

Let me illustrate my point. Imagine you won an award on your job, and the employer decided to hold a celebration banquet in your honor. They rented a banquet hall for hundreds of your guests. They provide you with a luxury hotel overnight stay and a chauffeur for the day. Then right before you enter the banquet hall to be seated up front in your special seat, they put another individual in your place. Can you imagine how you would feel? That is what God feels when we use his praise for other than to honor him and for what he has done.

I do not want to offend any searching, hungry soul, but I am honestly trying to shock you to the point of soberly thinking by using your brain, the one thing God has given us all. You see, God does not mind you thinking; he is simply concerned about you thinking with him being excluded from the process. Stop leaving your brain at the door of religion (the absence of thought). Stop letting intellect weigh you down when pursuing God (overthinking). Religion requires a reckless abandonment of your God-given faculties of the ability to think. Relationship requires a proper and productive use of them. This book is not at all an intellectual approach to intimacy with God, no more than two lovers being passionately drunk in each other's love only by their intellectual thought patterns. But it does involve the use of the area of your being called the brain, which houses your intellect and your emotions. One of the highest expressions of love is to love God with the part of your being called the mind, and he wants fullness of its capabilities. This includes creativity, problem solving, analytical ability, and thought processing.

Chapter Reflections and Notes

_____

_____

_____

_____

_____

_____

_____

_____

_____

_____

_____

_____

_____

_____

_____

_____

_____

chapter nine

The Wounded Souls and the Father Figure Syndrome

I was traveling in a major city in the United States, and I turned a corner and entered an area filled with the homeless and drug-addicted. There were various age groups and races, both males and females. This environment was nothing new to me because I grew up in the hood, or low-income areas. Except this time, the experience was like entering a world of wounded souls that were never healed. They possibly had some kind of experience in their lives that inflicted such a wound to the soul that brought them to this place. The difference between them and me was that they had checked out on life, becoming a nonfunctioning, wounded soul. I was a functioning wounded soul, able to live this life wounded by experiences without the use of the momentary assisted escapes of the drug or alcohol drink of choice. But I was wounded.

A wound to my soul dealt with my birth father. Before my stepdad came into the picture, I vividly remember while growing up as a child, when my cousins would talk about their dad, I would have to make up stories about mine. There are several stories as to why he was not in my life at all. All I know is that shortly after my birth, my mother moved from New York back to the South. While I was growing up, she promised me she would connect me to my biological father on my eighteenth birthday. This promise made absolutely no sense to me, but I grew up with no information and in the age of no Internet, so what could I do?

The matter became worse because around about the age of eighteen, I was lying on my bed half asleep, and I had a strange physical experience. It felt as though someone had put a gun to my head and pulled the trigger. I will never forget that experience. I would later be informed by my brother (on my biological father's side) that it was around that time our father shot himself in the head on his bed miles away in New York. This experience felt as though he had left me twice, once when I was born and then by suicide. This experience created years of imprisonment of what can be called the father figure syndrome. The importance of the father in a child's life is an understatement. In several cultures of society, the father has been removed from the family either systematically or voluntarily. The importance of both parents in the family structure is very significant. Both parents contribute their unique deposit into a child's life. If one of those deposits is left undone, the child could unconsciously search for it, possibly all his or her life. Those experiences leave gaps in the soul and cause questions from the heart. Why? Was I not good enough? Am I even lovable? Why did you do that to me, your child? What is wrong with me?

The start of the freedom from the father figure syndrome was when God used an older man to speak the following words into my life. "God wants to settle this father figure thing in your life once and for all! Do you want to know why you never had a father figure in your life? God could not trust what you are carrying on the inside of you in another man's hand." Wow! That answered a lot of questions for me. Often we do not realize what we are carrying. We do not know the value of our lives. Often we do not see why we were sent here until later in life, or we never discover it at all. If your value is so significant that God could not trust you in the hands of any other person, that speaks volumes of your value and worth! There are several examples in the Bible where this has occurred.

David, who was disowned by his natural father and was not even acknowledged as being a son. Moses, who was put in a basket and sent down the Nile River. Jesus (Yeshua), whose stepdad, Joseph, was there at the beginning of his life but was never heard of in his older years. You heard of his siblings like Jude and his mother. But where was Joseph? Ask yourself, "Am I carrying a purpose on the inside that I am not aware of yet?" God, the lover of your soul, has been and will always be the father figure you have unconsciously desired.

With this understanding, the help of my wife, and the lover of my soul (God), I have been able to heal those wounds of the soul. I remember vividly sitting on the side of my bed, crying like a child who couldn't find his mother, but I was a grown man. It finally hit me. Why did my birth father leave me twice, once when I was born and then when he committed suicide? Why did almost all of the few male role models I have had started good but then evolve into mistreatment? Those same questions began. Why? Was I not good enough? What is wrong with me? What did I do wrong? What started on the side of my bed ended on the floor as I angrily started pounding the concrete foundation of my house. You could hear the pounding from another room in the house. I did not know all that was inside of me. That was the release of my freedom from the wounds of my soul and the father figure syndrome.

We all have similar stories of wounds that are relatable. I can recall a story of an individual growing up in a household experiencing the environment of outbursts of rage. As I remember, several instances of these stories occurred in the late seventies through the early eighties. An example was when the individual was in the bedroom with their younger sister, and all of a sudden, there were loud sounds of yelling, things thrown around, and glass crashing and breaking. This commotion startled them as a young child, so they ran and hid in the closet as the noise continued. While hiding in the closet, they contemplated how they could get their younger sister to bring her from her crib to safety. After everything settled down, the mother came to get them out of the closet, and what they saw was like a miniature tornado had passed through that small apartment and tossed the entire contents around. This experience was one of their dad's fits of rage. How was a child supposed to process this? In elementary school, they would feel as though they had to rush home to protect the younger sister. The family moved to various locations in the region, but the fits of rage continued into middle school years and even high school.

I also remember a story of someone's similar experience of violent outbursts in the home. He described an account of hearing his mother's cry for help—a cry that said definitely something was wrong. Removing the weights off a five-pound steel curling bar, he proceeded down the hall to his mother's room with bar firmly gripped in hand. As he entered their bathroom, he saw his dad choking his mother in the bathtub. He swung the weight bar hard as he could. The bar somehow bounced off the head of his dad. This reaction was an act of God, thankfully, because the dad could have died, and the child could have possibly been in jail. But before you close the book on all these people, we have to realize they also had stories of inflicted wounds that never were healed. By no means are their actions excused, but it helps to see more clearly the why.

Whether you are a functioning or nonfunctioning wounded soul, the lover of your soul actively wants to heal all your wounds. An offended heart suffocates your passion. A wounded soul numbs your ability to feel the passion. These offenses and wounds can come in various forms, such as rejection, rape, molestation, disappointment, abandonment, abuse, unexpected or unwanted death of a loved one, and the like. The onslaught from the enemy of your soul can start as soon as you into this world. These wounds come by various bad experiences, from a high school breakup to a spousal affair, from cruel words to being falsely accused, from being made to feel you have no value to rejection. The list goes on.

One of the impactful tools to wound your soul is rejection. The purpose of rejection are to separate you from your full awareness of your worth. Rejection is intended to separate you from the only one who can reveal your full worth, the Creator (the lover of your soul). Rejection is the belly for the appetite of lust. It has a hunger that is incapable of being satisfied. Nonfunctioning wounded souls try to feed it with drugs and alcohol. Functioning wounded souls try to feed it with accomplishments, power, and sexuality, or they religiously ignore it. The soul-piercing effects of rejection stand in defiance to time and space, leaving all of us affected in some way. It is the arrow shot from a distance in Psalms 91:5 and then shows up centuries later, gaining closer proximity as the fiery dart in Ephesians 6:16. While living in this world, you may have an experience of your soul being wounded. But God (the lover of your soul) wants to heal them all. The New International Version translation of Psalm 34:18 says, "The Lord is close to the brokenhearted and saves those who are crushed in spirit," and Psalm 147:3 says, "He heals the brokenhearted and binds up their wounds." But he can heal only what you let him.

Chapter Reflections and Notes

chapter ten

The Fear Factor and
the Impasse

Fear strangles your ability to connect with God authentically. How are you going to get close to someone whom you fear? Fear means the uncomfortable feeling of being afraid of something or someone. How can a wife or girlfriend have a healthy, authentic connection with her significant other when she is afraid of him? How can a child have any meaningful relationship with a parent that rules by abuse and intimidation? You might agree that these situations would make it next to impossible to have a healthy, satisfying, and deeply connected relationship. You must understand that this also applies to our relationship with God. If we put up emotional walls and develop defense mechanisms to protect us from the fear of what others might do and say, then what kind of fortress would we build from the Almighty God? The emotional walls get more challenging to penetrate if we add in our beliefs and what we were taught.

Perhaps you can identify with the biblical statement, "It rains on the just as well as the unjust" (Matthew 5:45 KJV). It is as if God is in heaven dispensing all types of calamities and tribulations on evil as well as the good people. In fact, rain is beneficial for everyone. We must have rain to grow crops for food. We must have rain to hydrate our bodies, which are over 90 percent water. The rain benefits every living thing on this planet. Let us look at the scripture in context: "For that will reveal your identity as children of your heavenly Father. He is kind to all by bringing the sunrise to warm and rainfall to refresh whether a person does what is good or evil" (Matthew 5:45 TPT).

Perhaps you also believe and have been taught that no man can look at God and live. In context, the scripture has recorded:

> Then He said ... "I will be gracious to whom I will be gracious, and I will have compassion on whom I will have compassion." But He said, "You cannot see My face; for no man shall see Me, and live." And the Lord said, "Here is a place by Me, and you shall stand

on the rock. So, it shall be, while My glory passes by, that I will put you in the cleft of the rock and will cover you with My hand while I pass by. Then I will take away My hand, and you shall see My back; but My face shall not be seen." (Exodus 33: 20–23 NKJV)

So, Moses got to see God but not his face. Jacob did too. "And Jacob called the name of the place Peniel: for I have seen God face to face, and my life is preserved" (Genesis 32:30 KJV). What realistic passionate pursuit of seeking his face, as the scripture instructs us to do, can be maintained, especially with result of doing so means you die, as some translations suggest?

In fact, there are several occurrences in the Bible where other human beings got to see the Creator. In theology, these are called the theophanies of God: The way God shows up different times in the Bible is the visible manifestation of his deity. Abraham got to eat a meal with the Savior before he was even born of a virgin birth. In Genesis 18:1–5, it states,

The Lord appeared again to Abraham near the oak grove belonging to Mamre. One day Abraham was sitting at the entrance to his tent during the hottest part of the day. He looked up and noticed three men standing nearby. When he saw them, he ran to meet them and welcomed them, bowing low to the ground. "My lord," he said, "if it pleases you, stop here for a while. Rest in the shade of this tree while water is brought to wash your feet. And since you've honored your servant with this visit, let me prepare some food to refresh you before you continue on your journey. (NLT)

So, what does it really mean to not be able to look at God or his face? Being presented with the possibility of seeing God in his glorified state that would result in your death destroys any desire for your full pursuit of him.

Fear will kill any possibility of experiencing the highest levels of the intimacy with your Creator. There must be an adjusting our view of experiencing his presence. Again, anything or anyone that comes to kill, steal, or destroy any beneficial aspect of your life, especially your spiritual life, is not coming from the lover of your soul (God). "For God hath not given us the spirit of fear; but of power, and of love, and of a sound mind" (2 Timothy 1:7 KJV). "Love never brings fear, for fear is always related to punishment. But love's perfection drives the fear of punishment far from our hearts. Whoever walks constantly afraid of punishment has not reached love's perfection" (1 John 4:18 TPT).

An impasse is defined as "a predicament (or situation) affording no obvious escape."[22] This understanding is like a road that is blocked by some object, keeping you from your destination. Some of us have impasses that are not as obvious as other issues that we have conquered in our lives. They could be the residue from bad childhood experiences, bad relationships, negative statements, inner vows, or failures injected into our souls to keep us from being whole and from being emotionally connected. To further tighten the power of the grip of these impasses, some of us were taught the following two belief statements:

As long as we live in this fallen world in the fallen bodies, we will have to go through negative situations. Jesus (Yeshua) offers us a way pass the impasse, saying,

> I have told you these things, so that in Me you may have [perfect] peace. In the world you have [there is] tribulation and distress and suffering, but be courageous [be confident, be undaunted, be filled with joy]; I have overcome the world. [My conquest is

---

[22] Merriam-Webster (2004).

accomplished, My victory abiding.] (John
16:33 AMP)

He also stated,

They (those that believe on me) are not of
the world, just as I am not of the world.
Sanctify them by Your truth. Your word is
truth. (John 17:16–17 NKJV)

As believers, we are supposed to replicate what is
going on in heaven! Are there attacks of the enemy going
on in heaven? Is anybody developing cancer, lupus, or
Alzheimer's in heaven? Is there any impoverished area
in the city of heaven? Why was he born, if we are to go
through all the things we would have gone through had he
simply stayed in heaven? What kind of abundant life did
he really bring to us that believe in him?

The second belief statement is God is allowing horrible
situations to come upon you to try your faith. To say that
God is testing or trying you in an area may be a wrongful
assumption, implying that he has to allow you to go to a
situation to see what you will and will not do. Question:
When did God stop being omniscient? When did he stop
being the one true and all-wise God who knows everything?
Is he all-knowing until he gets to you? Or does he know

everything there is to know except when it comes to you? And then he has to allow hardship upon you to figure you out? God forbid.

It is not the heavenly Father's desire that we walk around in this fragmented type of existence. He desires to heal every area of our lives, including the areas that we are not aware of, including the areas of our beliefs. The heavenly Father, the lover of your soul, is intentional and purposeful in the mending of broken hearts of any individual who cries out for help. But just as a mother can tell the difference in the cry for help of a child, so can God. There is an ordinary cry for help from a child, and then there is a cry for help from a child where the child is in "a predicament (situation) affording no obvious escape." This situation is a problem. This is a dangerous situation. Most mothers can distinguish this distinctive cry in their child's voice. I witnessed this with my wife and our first newborn. There were times when our child would cry, and my wife asked me to check the baby's diaper or check to see if he was hungry. On the other hand, there were instances when my wife would jump straight out of her sleep based on the sound of our child's cry. Her response usually woke me up and startled me in the process.

I believe God has installed this trait in women as a direct resemblance of a character trait that he has toward us. Therefore, the question is when you cry out to God, which cry is distinctively heard? Is it the cry that is only in need of milk, or is it the cry that causes him to respond from his throne immediately? Hebrews 5:13–14 declares,

> For every spiritual infant who lives on milk is not yet pierced by the revelation of righteousness [the character of God]. But solid food is for the mature, whose spiritual senses perceive heavenly matters. And they have been adequately trained by what they've experienced to emerge with understanding of the difference between what is truly excellent and what is evil and harmful. (TPT)

This is why I believe it is wise to do a spiritual and belief examination of ourselves at least once a year. Most of us will visit our dentist, optometrist, and primary doctor for designated annual checkups and exams. We will even take our vehicles in for a tune-up and oil change. But how often do we do a personal examination of our spiritual condition? The Word of God clearly instructs us to "evaluate yourselves to see whether you are in *the* faith and living your lives as [committed] believers. Examine yourselves [not me]! Or do you not recognize this about yourselves [by an ongoing experience] that Jesus Christ is in you" (2 Corinthians 13:5 AMP). At some point in time, you must break out of the wilderness of suffering before your life dies at the gate of the promises of God. If the enemy can have you in love with suffering and hardships long enough until you die, or the Lord Jesus comes back having not experienced the promises, that would be like having no promises at all. If there is an impasse, "a predicament (situation) affording no obvious escape," in your soul, it is not because of the lover of your soul, who is eagerly waiting to respond to your earnest cry.

Chapter Reflections and Notes

chapter eleven

The Deceptive Acts of Love

Just because people perform acts of love or demonstrate their love for you by their actions, that does not necessarily mean that they have love. A person's actions alone are not the only and complete litmus test to determine their present possession of love or their real character. This truth is applicable to a person's love for you, your love toward others, and your intimate love toward God, the lover of your soul. Although it is true that God is the discerner of the intentions and motives of the heart, he can also inform you of the motives and conditions of your heart.

The church has initiated the formula of consistent attendance plus faithful tithe and giving equals good character and love. This formula is dangerous and faulty. This is one of the greatest deceptions that has been perpetuated in the church. This formula has replaced the lack of real ability to discern the heart and motives (fruit of the spirit). In the "love section" of the Bible, 1 Corinthians 13, this concept of deceptive acts of love is described. It states, "If I were to be so generous as to give away everything [everything] I owned to feed the poor, and to offer my body to be burned as a martyr, without the pure motive of love, I would gain nothing of value" (TPT).

It would be an educated guess to say some have infiltrated the ranks of the church and even placed in positions of authority based on this faulty system of faithfulness and giving. The result is the fulfillment of one of the parables of Jesus in Matthew 13:24–28. Jesus taught us, saying,

> Heaven's kingdom realm can be compared to a farmer who planted good seed in his field. But at night, when everyone [the church] was asleep, an enemy came and planted poisonous weeds among the wheat and ran away. When the wheat sprouted and bore grain, the weeds also appeared. So, the farmer's hired hands came to him and said, 'Sir, wasn't that good seed that you sowed in the field? Where did all these weeds come from?' "He answered, 'This has to be the work of an enemy. (TPT)

Notice what he said: the people assigned the care were asleep. I am not saying that you should not be faithful, nor am I saying that you should not give. We are instructed to do such. But the why and how you show acts of love should be honestly examined for pure acts of love out of the biblical definition of love. Jesus (Yeshua) declared in Luke 11:42, 44,

> You Pharisees are hopeless frauds! For you are obsessed with peripheral issues, like paying meticulous tithes on the smallest herbs that grow in your gardens. These matters you should do. Yet … you ignore the most important duty of all: to walk in the love of God. Re-adjust your values and place first things first. "You Pharisees, what hopeless frauds! Your true character is hidden, like an unmarked grave that hides the corruption inside, defiling all who come in contact with you." (TPT)

When it comes to experiencing an intimate love for God, the lover of our souls, how do we know that what we are experiencing is genuine? By making sure our motives or our why is pure; more importantly when he begins to share how he feels, and you feel it.

One of the most thought-provoking scriptures in the Bible to me is recorded in Matthew 7:22–23, "Many will say to me in that day, Lord, Lord, have we not prophesied in thy name? and in thy name have cast out devils? and in thy name done many wonderful works? And then will I profess unto them, I never knew you: depart from me, ye that work iniquity" (KJV). Another translation says, "Lord, Lord, don't you remember us? Didn't we cast out demons and do many miracles for the sake of your name?' But I will have to say to them, 'Go away from me ... I've never been joined [intimate] to you!'" (TPT). Let us be honest. If you were to see someone to perform some miracle, like raising the dead or opening blinded eyes, most people would say that person knows God. But Jesus is saying in the previous text that it's not necessarily true. The word *know* or *joined* in these texts implies a certain level of intimacy. For example, you may say you know a particular movie star or celebrity, but really you do not know them. You know of them. Such people have never intimately shared their concerns and deepest feelings with you. Realistically, you do not know them. On the other hand, you may have a certain level of intimacy with your spouse, parents, family members, and very close friends. That is the result of experiences that have been shared and felt.

So how will you know when you are so intimately connected with God in such a way? How do you avoid hearing those horrible words, "I never knew you," that he will be forced to say to some on that final day? When you sincerely go after God in such a way that he begins to expose how he feels, and you feel it! Then you have evolved in such a way that God knows you, and you know him. Such a level of intimacy only happens based on the level of closeness you have. It would be very strange and awkward if you walked up to your favorite celebrity and try to get them to share deep sentiments of the heart. They do not know you like that! The closer and more personal the relationship is, the more vulnerability and exposure that occurs. It is the same thing with God, the lover of your soul.

There is a story of a man who had a horrible dream of someone kidnapping his young son. The pain was so real in the dream that he yelled out a heart-wrenching sound that awakened his startled wife. But with prayer and his son growing up to be a man, he discovered that God was not trying to warn him. God had exposed his feelings to him. The pain the man felt in that dream is what we make God feel. It is what he feels when we go after everything else but him. It is what he feels when you preferred to be in the presence of your favorite celebrity rather than be in his presence. It is what he feels when we do things that we should not do. You see, sin is not just about going to heaven or hell, or when you are doing something wrong. It is more about every time we do something wrong, we are causing him the type of pain in this man's dream. Until all your mind, your soul, and your heart loves God—and this includes the area of your soul that houses your feelings—you are in jeopardy of him not knowing you. "But if anyone loves God ... he is known by Him [as His very own and is greatly loved]" (1 Corinthians 8:3 AMP).

Chapter Reflections and Notes

Section Three

The Solutions to Intimacy with God

chapter twelve

The Secret Place

There is a very familiar extract of scripture, and most believers can quote sections of it: it is Psalms 91. This scripture paints a picture that speaks of a particular place in which believers can have experiences that have multiple benefits—benefits of protection, benefits of avoidance of trickery, benefits of not being affected by disasters, and so on. Let us read it in context.

> He who dwells in the secret place of the Most High Shall abide under the shadow of the Almighty. I will say of the Lord, "He is my refuge and my fortress; My God, in Him I will trust." Surely, He shall deliver you from the snare of the fowler And from the perilous pestilence. He shall cover you with His feathers,

And under His wings you shall take refuge; His truth shall be your shield and buckler. You shall not be afraid of the terror by night, Nor of the arrow that flies by day, Nor of the pestilence that walks in darkness, Nor of the destruction that lays waste at noonday. (Psalm 91:1–6 NKJV)

With all these benefits, one would think anybody would logically want to know how to receive these benefits.

If you approach this from a purely religious point of view, you will miss the whole point and observe only this particular text with all the symbolism and metaphors and leave it at that. But, if you approach this from an understanding of a relationship, you will understand that the Word of God is painting a picture of a specifically individualize place and moment; it is so individualized that it is the equivalent of our fingerprints. Not only is it tailored and personalized, but it is also secretive. The secrecy of "the secret place" is similar to the secrecy of the intimate bedroom of a husband and wife. There are private things that go on between a husband and wife in that place at those moments that generally nobody else on the planet knows. In the same manner, there is a secret place God has designed specifically for each one of us. Some of us may have more than one secret place. Where is your secret place, and how do you discover it?

Even prayer, our two-way communication with the heavenly Father, is supposed to have some level of secrecy. One of the savior's teaching on prayer is recorded in Matthew 6:6, "But you, when you pray, go into your room, and when you have shut your door, pray to your Father who is in the secret place; and your Father who sees in secret will reward you openly" (NJKV). The initial goal of prayer (communication with God) is to eventually grow to the place in prayer where you grow to know the voice of God. This understanding is the same approach as a couple starting in a relationship. The more they communicate, the more they easily recognize the voice of the other. Before the advancement of caller ID on the phone, you had to identify the person based on knowing their voice. You could not see them, and all you had was their voice on the other end of the call. In prayer, you can grow in the same way. You may not yet see him, but you can grow to recognize his voice. John 10:3–5 explains.

> The sheep recognize the voice of the true
> Shepherd, for he calls his own by name and
> leads them out, for they belong to him. And
> when he has brought out all his sheep, he

walks ahead of them and they will follow him, for they are familiar with his voice. But they will run away from strangers and never follow them because they know it's the voice of a stranger. (TPT)

But to grow to the highest form of prayer means to return to the original form of prayer that the first humans had. Adam was so close to his Creator that he heard his footsteps walking in the Garden of Eden. Even immediately after the fall, Adam, Eve, and their son Cain communicated with God. God posed several rhetorical questions to each of them. Those experiences were not some deep feeling of just knowing, or some random statement or song played on the radio that seemed to provide some answer to their communication with God. He actually talked to them, and they heard him clearly. Prayer is a dialog not a monolog. It is a two-way conversation between you and God (the lover of your soul). But, modern day prayer consist of us doing the talking, asking, and that is the end of the conversation. We leave no time for God to say anything. That is like calling someone on the phone, starting the conversation then immediately hang up on the individual once finished. How odd of a conversation is that? Yet, it is done every Sunday at church and during personal times of prayer.

This understanding may take some adjusting to what you do, understand, believe, and were taught.

Also, let us take a scriptural examination of the removal of any atmospheric hindrances from the enemy of your soul when it comes to answered prayer (conversations with God). Do you know and believe that all such things have been removed? What if atmospheric oppositional hindrances from the forces of darkness were destroyed? Maybe this is a difficult thing to wrestle with if all you were taught, believed, and experienced was the "Daniel Experience," found in Daniel 10:12–14. This story describes the hindrance to Daniel's prayer by the forces of darkness. To further reinforce this belief, the concept of Satan still being the "prince of the air" is taught in Ephesians 2:2. The Jewish tradition describes this region as only being from the ground to the top of our atmosphere were oxygen (air) runs out. That is why the word air is included in his description. But a prince is always subjugated to the rule of the king's authority. Jesus (Yeshua, the King of kings) came with his death, burial, and resurrection, destroying such hindering forces of the enemy of your communication with God. In Matthew, Jesus said, "All authority (all power of absolute rule) in heaven and on earth has been given to Me" (Matthew 28:18 AMP). In Romans 10:17, it says, "Faith comes by hearing, and hearing by the word of God"

(NKJV). Without faith, it is virtually impossible to please God. If your faith is birthed through your ability to hear the voice of God, the lover of your soul, it is beneficial for both you and God if such hindrances are removed. Maybe the only hindrance is you and your beliefs.

Times of prayer and meditation on the Word of God can be two indicators pointing us in the right direction of the secret place. But let's not limit it to those because quite frankly, that is no secret. If you were to give me a few minutes while you were praying in your closet or private room, eventually I would find you, and the secrecy would be gone. Unhindered prayer and meditation on the Word of God are things we do in the secret place, but they are not the secret place of the Most High God. That secret place is not solely based on some confined private physical location. That may be a physical secret place. But what we are after is the discovery of "the secret place of the Most High God" as mentioned in Psalm 91:1–6. So, where and what is that secret place? Take note of this. When you feel God's presence the strongest and hear his voice the clearest, make a mental note of the following: Where are you? What time is it? What are you doing? The reason to make a mental note of it is to keep it a secret. This secret place is between you and your Creator. This secret place may include the use of sensory deprivation in a quiet place.

After the discovery of your initial secret place, do not be limited to just one secret place. There could possibly be more than just one secret place for you. This would give you the ability to choose the best secret place based on the moment. It would also help in maneuvering above the enemy's tactics.

Chapter Reflections and Notes

chapter thirteen

Created Access: The Belly, The Silver Cord, and The Anointing Oil

At creation, the Creator created us in such a way that would allow him to have access to us and us to have access to him, to keep and grow in connection and communication with him. Science is now discovering some of the amazing things that had already been laid out in the Word of God thousands of years before. Together we will examine the physical and scientific things about our being that were designed to develop and maintain a connection and closeness with the Creator. In order to connect with God, we must realize who we are dealing with and the ways and means by which we can connect with him.

I have an old friend whom I had been trying to connect with for years without any success. I knew who the person was, but I did not know the ways and means by which to connect with him. I did not know his phone number or address. I tried to find him on Facebook and the like with no success. First, I must understand who my friend is. This is crucially important; otherwise, I could be talking to the wrong person. This is the same thing when it comes to God the Father. We must know exactly who he is and the means and ways by which we can connect to him. This book is not intended or written to be a source for religious, philosophical, or scientific debate. Its sole purpose is to serve as a resource for the discovery and establishment of an intimate personal relationship with the Creator, the lover of your soul. But, we must at least scratch the surface of some of those deep thoughts in the quest to discover who God is.

Are all religions the same? On the surface, it may seem that all religions are similar, but as you go deeper, there are some fundamental exclusive differences. Let us simply deal with the names. The biblical account calls him Yahweh. The name is important because your name is part of the ingredients that create your identity and who you are. My long-lost friend whom I was searching for eventually ended up finding me on Facebook. After over twenty-five years, we were able to connect again over the phone. Now, let's say for an example that after twenty-five years, we were excited to talk to each other and catch up on some old times, but I started calling him names that were not his. What do you think my friend would do? He probably would have hung up and thought I was acting very strange. Why? Because he knows his name and his identity. If we, as mere human beings, have a clear understanding and knowledge of our name and our identity, why would we think God does not know his? If God does not know his name, his identity, then how will he be able to help us at critical times and in critical issues of our lives?

Now, let us go further down the path to the discovery of the truth of who he is. There has to be only one God, the Supreme Being. God would cease being the Supreme Being (highest in rank and authority) because there are others just like him. I will have to end this brief theological, philosophical, and religious discussion for now. But if you are still on your quest and discovery of who God is, I will leave you with these valuable resources. Dr. William Lane Craig, at www.reasonablefaith.org. Also Answers In Genesis, at www.answersingenesis.org/answers/, are great resources in your search. They also have YouTube channels with a wealth of knowledge. These resources will help those grappling with questions like, "Who is God? Who am I? Why am I here? Why does God let evil things happen?" The discovery and clarity of the answers to these common questions from humanity, ultimately will come through an intimate relationship with your creator. There are also some other great resources listed in the back of this book. For those of us who have already discovered the "who" of who God is, let us continue down the path at hand: the experiencing of a connected and intimate personal relationship with Yahweh (the God of the Bible).

It is a general understanding that God is a spiritual being. The Bible recorded in John 4:24, "God is a Spirit: and they that worship him must worship him in spirit and in truth" (KJV).

The description is apparent in determining what God is. He is a spirit, but that is no different than me searching for my friend on Facebook and discovering there are many people with his name. Which one is my friend? That takes some searching out and handling of factual truths. John 4:24 further gives instructions in this by saying to connect with God, it must be done "in spirit and in truth" (KJV). We now understand that God is a spirit, and we must connect with him spirit to spirit and our spirit to his spirit. But how are we supposed to do that when the church and the modern culture offer no clear definition of our spirit and location? Or when we are offered a vague description like "some force or energy within us"? How are we to locate and then connect our spirit with God's spirit with such unclear concepts?

Most of us are aware of a gut instinct, that feeling of something just not being right in the face of information, lack of knowledge, or circumstances; some call it intuition. A simple Internet search can deliver a flood of intuition gone wrong and examples of intuition (gut instinct) that saved lives from death and destruction. Not knowing the complete variables of any of those examples, the purpose here is to discover the possibility of the location where our bodies and spirits connect. In the 1990s, a prominent doctor by the name of Michael Gershon made a starling scientific rediscovery in his book *The Second Brain*.[23] During our early stage of development in our mothers' wombs, our nervous system separates into two parts. One part goes to the head, forming the brain and the central nervous system. The other part goes to the area of the belly (abdominal area) and forms the enteric nervous system. The enteric nervous system is thought to have potent influence on the brain and central nervous system. The brain and the central nervous system then control every act and function of the body.

The Bible paints an even more descriptive picture of the connecting location between our physical and spiritual

---

[23] Gershon, M. (1998).

being, unlike those unclear concepts previously mentioned. The scripture records in John 7:38, "He that believeth on me, as the scripture hath said, out of his belly (abdominal area) shall flow rivers of living water" (KJV). In another translation, it records, "He who believes in Me [who adheres to, trusts in, and relies on Me], as the Scripture has said, 'From his innermost being will flow continually rivers of living water'" (AMP). The Bible gets even more precise in locating where the physical body could possibly connect with the spirit. "Earnestly remember your Creator before the silver cord [of life] is broken ... then the dust [out of which God made man's body] will return to the earth as it was, and the spirit will return to God who gave it" (Ecclesiastes 12:6–7 AMP).

So, if the Word of God points to the abdominal region, to where our innermost being can be, and there is a silver cord that connects our body to our spirit, this is amazing! Where else do we see this system? It's in our mothers' wombs when we are forming. The Creator used the same system of physical connection we have in the womb to our mother to connect our physical being to our spiritual being. We are connected physically to our mothers in the abdominal region by a cord called an umbilical cord. In the same way, we are connected to our spirit in the abdominal area by a silver cord.

Did you know that your body and mind go through a preserving process that starts in your brain? Your brain secretes an oily substance that is similar to olive oil. It starts in your brain and then goes down your spinal cord, to be distributed throughout your body and central nervous system. Part of the oil turns white and goes to the pineal gland; the rest of it continues its journey through your spinal cord to the rest of your body with its life-giving substance. This oil has a fishy smell. There are several things that stand out here. First, the smell is fishy, or that of a fish—one of the symbols of Christ. Second, the process of this oily substance starts in the brain, exemplifying the scripture in Psalms 23:5, "You prepare a table before me in the presence of my enemies; You anoint my head with oil; My cup runs over" (NKJV). The process of anointing started with shepherds. They would pour oil on the head of the sheep to keep insects from entering the ears, dulling the hearing, and eventually killing the sheep. Perhaps this was an early outward example of what happens spiritually and the purpose of this oily process. Third, the scientific community named this oil substance Khristos. This word is an ancient Greek word for Christ. Scientists could have called this oil any other scientific word that is hard to pronounce. But they named it the Christ oil, the oil of the anointed one. Last, it is God (Yahweh) who does this anointing process as recorded in scripture. "But the anointing which you have received from Him abides in you, and you do not need that anyone teach you; but as the same anointing teaches you concerning all things, and is true, and is not a lie, and just as it has taught you, you will abide in Him" (1 John 2:27 NKJV).

Chapter Reflections and Notes

chapter fourteen

The Dreams, Visions, and Encounters

I used to think that God created sleep for rest and to restore the body. I am starting to believe that the primary motive for God creating sleep is to have uninterrupted, clear communication with us. This understanding is indicated in the Bible.

> In a dream, in a vision of the night, When deep sleep falls upon men, While slumbering on their beds, Then He opens the ears of men, And seals their instruction. In order to turn man from his deed, And conceal pride from man, He keeps back his soul from the Pit, And his life from perishing by the sword. (Job 33:15–18 NKJV)

This example is exemplified when Joseph was warned in a dream in Matthew 2:13. "Now when they had departed, behold, an angel of the Lord appeared to Joseph in a dream, saying, 'Arise, take the young Child and His mother, flee to Egypt, and stay there until I bring you word; for Herod will seek the young Child to destroy Him'" (NKJV). There are several other examples in the Bible, like Samuel in 1 Samuel 3:7–10.

> Samuel had no experience with Yahweh [God], because the word of Yahweh had not yet been revealed to him. Yahweh called Samuel a third time. Samuel got up, went to Eli, and said, "Here I am. You called me." Then Eli realized that Yahweh was calling the boy. "Go, lie down," Eli told Samuel. "When he calls you, say, 'Speak, Yahweh. I'm listening.'" So, Samuel went and lay down in his room. Yahweh [God] came and stood there. He called as he had called the other times: "Samuel!" And Samuel replied, "Speak. I'm listening. (GW/NOG)

When we are awake, our conscious minds are distracted by the processing of millions of pieces of information per second, performing tasks, and caring for the things of this world that the voice of God is either silenced or drowned out. Maybe that is why it is called the still small voice. Sleep is a form of natural sedation where parts of the brain shut down or quiet down. This allows God's communication with us to be more noticeable. This is true whether medically or naturally induced sleep occurs. I remember a few years ago when I had to be put to sleep by an anesthesiologist to have all four of my wisdom teeth removed. As I slowly gained consciousness, I could hear my oral surgeon say, "He must be a preacher or something." Still under heavy sedation, I heard myself quoting Psalms 23:4, "Yea, though I walk through the valley of the shadow of death, I will fear no evil; For You are with me; Your rod and Your staff, they comfort me" (NJKV). I was thankful for the modernization of anesthesiology started on October 16, 1846, in "the Ether Dome" at Harvard School of Medicine. But it was not until recent years (the late 2000s) that scientists begin to study what happens to a person when medically induced to sleep (sedation, etc.). It seems the only part of the brain that remains active during this time is the auditory cortex, which is responsible for processing sound.[24] Science proved again what was already revealed in the Word of God. The story is recorded in Mark 5:38–42.

---

[24] Black Box, Radiolab, WNYC studios. (n.d.).

Then He (Jesus) came to the house of the ruler of the synagogue and saw a tumult and those who wept and wailed loudly (they thought the child was dead). When He came in, He said to them, "Why make this commotion and weep? The child is not dead but sleeping." And they ridiculed Him ... he took the child by the hand, and said to her, "Talitha, cumi," which is translated, "Little girl, I say to you, arise." Immediately the girl arose and walked ... And they were overcome with great amazement. (Mark 5:38-42 NKJV)

Natural sleep or sedation has similar properties and activities. In fact, scientists call the state of the brain just before you fall asleep and when you are relaxed with your eyes closed the alpha state. When you go into this alpha state, just before you fall completely asleep, the Alpha and Omega shows up. He shows up to do what is described in Job 33:16, to download secured instructions.

Takeaway:

- Believe the Creator can and wants to speak to you in your dreams.

- Verbally give only Yahweh the lover of your soul permission to speak to you in dreams and visions.

- Ask him to guard your heart, spirit, and mind with his peace, as in Philippians 4:6–7.

- "Get a notepad and pen, or download a note-taking app, to keep by your bed for recording your night visions (dreams) and communications."

  The Word of God instructs, "Write the vision And engrave it plainly on [clay] tablets So that the one who reads it will run. "For the vision is yet for the appointed [future] time It hurries toward the goal [of fulfillment]; it will not fail." (Habakkuk 2:2-3 AMP) Sometimes when reviewing your documented record of these dreams and night visions, you might discover a pattern to an answer!

- Keeping these notes shows God (the lover of your soul) you take what he has to say as important and meaningful. If you do not treat them as such, why should he reveal any other communications? Perhaps this maybe the key to our seemingly list of unanswered prayers. We have been waiting for answers and guidance for this or that, and the answer was previously given in our dreams that were not recorded. Selah.

- Anything that is communicated will always agree with the Scriptures (the Word of God).

Chapter Reflections and Notes

chapter fifteen

The Purpose and Benefits of Fasting and Prayer

Fasting is a word that is experiencing popularity in modern culture, but not for the purposes we will discuss in this book. Today there have been types of created fasting that have nothing to do with fasting at all. You may have heard people say they are fasting from social media, my morning coffee, or some guilty pleasure. All these may have good intentions and benefits, but they are not fasting. They are simply lifestyle changes. According to *Webster's Dictionary of 1828*, fasting is defined as abstaining from eating food.[25] A few years ago, fasting was a word that people would have a distaste for, or they would connect it with some religious and spiritual fanaticism. Today, fasting has been made culturally popular in the health

---

[25] Webster, N. (2015).

industry by the term *intermittent fasting*. This form of fasting involves not eating during certain times of the day. Though intermittent fasting may have some healthy physical and mental benefits, this is only part of the importance of biblical fasting. There is a biblical story where Jesus (Yeshua) described the importance of biblical fasting, and it is recorded in Matthew 17:19–21.

> Later the disciples came to him privately and asked, "Why couldn't we cast out the demon?" He told them, "It was because of your lack of faith. I promise you, if you have faith inside of you no bigger than the size of a small mustard seed, you can say to this mountain, 'Move away from here and go over there,' and you will see it move! There is nothing you couldn't do! But this kind of demon is cast out only through prayer and fasting. (TPT)

Jesus (Yeshua) fasted, Moses fasted, Elijah fasted, Esther fasted, Daniel fasted, Nehemiah fasted, John the Baptist fasted, Peter fasted, Paul fasted, and other people in the Bible fasted. Ezra fasted for a divine strategy on how to transport over seven thousand pounds of gold and over twenty tons of silver along a path of thieves and robbers to Jerusalem. Surely there has to be some significant importance to fasting and prayer. But what is the biblical purpose of abstaining from what your body naturally needs?

The purpose of prayer and fasting is not to get God to move on your behalf, or even to get a blessing. All those things are eagerly and already provided. Second Corinthians 1:20 declares, "For all the promises of God in Him are Yes, and in Him Amen, to the glory of God through us" (NJKV). Second Peter 1:3–4 further declares,

> Everything we could ever need for life and complete devotion to God has already been deposited in us by his divine power. For all things needed for this life are lavished upon us through the rich experience of [intimacy] knowing him. He intimately calls us by name and invites us to come to him through a glorious manifestation of his goodness. As a result of this, he has given you magnificent promises that are beyond all price, so that through the power of these tremendous promises you can experience partnership with the divine nature, by which you have

escaped the corrupt desires that are of the world. (TPT)

Therefore, the purpose of fasting and prayer is to put your being back into proper alignment to be able to hear God's instructions regarding what he will do and to experience the blessings and promises that are already provided. If we are honest and humble, most of us are experiencing this life in the "mind to body" mode or the "body to mind" mode. This type of functioning is not only out of alignment but also eliminates the use of your spirit. Starting at childhood, we have to be taught how to function from mind to body. Billy, get down; you will hurt yourself. Little Jessica do not go over there; it is dangerous. All those types of statements may be good and beneficial, but they plunge us into the misalignment of our beings. These modes of mind to body functioning are all left brain to body, or rational fear. The original proper alignment of our beings is in this order: spirit to right brain, right brain to left brain, left brain to body. The purpose of fasting and prayer is to realign our beings back into proper alignment, where God's spirit connects to our spirits and governs the rest of our being.

How do you fast? First of all, it is recommended that you seek the advice of your physician before starting any form of fasting. Some people start in small increments: cut out one meal a day, then an entire day with no food, then work up to consecutive days of fasting. Whichever you choose to commit yourself, include with your time of biblical fasting prayer and studying the Bible. Drink at least eight glasses of water per day and maybe some herbal tea. Choose one single reason for each period of your time of fasting. It initially should be to get closer and more intimate with God, the lover of your soul. Also, find your secret place as outlined in chapter 12.

What happens when you fast? With fasting, you can expect the unexpected. As stated earlier in this chapter, when you abstain from food for any lengthy time period, your mind and body will be at odds with each other. Your body will be getting rid of toxins and old waste while at the same time communicating to your brain a request for more food. You are breaking the routine and habit of communication between the brain and body only. This breaking of connection is not just the natural habit of the eating; it is also the times and amounts you would routinely eat. This breaking of communication starts around the third day for most people.

Chapter Reflections and Notes

chapter sixteen

The Communion Revelation and Communion Fasting

The religious ceremony of partaking of the communion is a church ordinance most believers know. It involves the consumption of bread (or Jewish unleavened bread) and wine (or kosher grape juice) as portrayed in Luke 22:17-20. But this experience was never intended to be a religious ceremony. The history of communion was a part of the Jewish celebration of the Passover, the Jewish feast of God delivering them from the slavery of the Egyptians and protection from the spirit of death. It was done in the intimacy of their homes. Jesus (Yeshua) shares this intimate experience with his disciples before his death in a private room. But before that intimate experience, he had this public confrontation with a crowd and religious leaders.

These words of Jesus sparked an angry outburst among the Jews. They protested, saying, "Does this man expect us to eat his body?" Jesus replied to them, "Listen to this eternal truth: Unless you eat the body of the Son of Man and drink his blood, you will not have eternal life. Eternal life comes to the one who eats my body and drinks my blood, and I will raise him up in the last day. *For my body is real food for your spirit and my blood is real drink.* The one who eats my body and drinks my blood lives in me and I live in him. The Father of life sent me, and he is my life. In the same way, the one who feeds upon me, I will become his life. I am not like the bread your ancestors ate and later died. I am the living Bread that comes from heaven. Eat this Bread and you will live forever! (John 6:52–58 TPT)

Obviously, he was not talking about cannibalism. After all, for the communion experience he had with his disciples, there was no consuming of his actual body or blood. But as the intimate experience unfolded, he said these profound statements: "And as they were eating, Jesus took bread, blessed and broke it, and gave it to the disciples and said, 'Take, eat; this is My body.' Then He took the cup, and gave thanks, and gave it to them, saying, 'Drink from it, all of you. For this is my blood of the new covenant, which is shed for many for the remission of sins'" (Matthew 26:26–28 NKJV).

When we partake of the communion, we are consuming his resurrected body and New Covenant blood. This understanding must be grasped. You must adapt the belief that the communion feeds your spirit. For he declared, "My body is real food for your spirit." If his body is food for your spirit and you only consume the communion once a month or less, how malnourished or anorexic is your spirit? If you were to feed your physical body once a month, how do you think that would turn out? We must make the life change to consume the communion daily, or more often if possible, remembering what he has provided. His statement "This is my body, this my blood" indicates that somehow by faith, he converts the bread and the wine into his body and blood.

Such transformations would not be the first time he would change natural substances into something else. After all, the first miracle we know of was him turning water into wine. If he can change water to wine, then why can't he change wine to his blood? In the wilderness, he supernaturally caused sweet bread in the form of wafers (manna) to fall from the heavens to feed the children of Israel. Because he can cause bread to fall from the heavens, which was a type and shadow of himself (the bread of life) coming down from heaven, surely he can convert the wafer of bread that we consume during communion to his body. If he can deliver food the angels ate (manna) to his people on earth, surely he can convert the bread of communion into his body. The children of Israel ate food from heaven as recorded in Psalm 78:23–25. "He had commanded the clouds above, And opened the doors of heaven, Had rained down manna on them to eat, And given them of the bread of heaven. Men ate angels' food; He sent them food to the full" (NJKV). From his own mouth, Jesus [Yeshua] then says, "This loaf is my body … This cup is my blood of the new covenant I make with you" (Luke 22:19–20 TPT).

Most believers were taught a fear-based understanding of the communion experience. The knowledge passed from generations was that you must make sure your heart is right with God and your sins are confessed before the communion, or you eat and drink damnation on yourself. I do believe that a level of respect should be exercised when consuming communion, but this fear-based doctrine has had a negative impact on the communion intentions. If the fear-based doctrine taught to us was true, then none of the disciples could consume the communion. They were all sinners! The Savior (Jesus) had not been crucified and risen from the dead yet. Just hours later, Peter would curse the crowd out and deny he ever knew the Savior. Let us look at the actual text in context.

> But let a man examine himself, and so let him eat of the bread and drink of the cup. For he who eats and drinks in an unworthy manner eats and drinks judgment to himself, not discerning the Lord's body. For this reason, many are weak and sick among you, and many sleep. (1 Corinthians 11:28–30 NKJV)

The word *discerning* in this text is a mental activity and not a lifestyle behavior. In other words, by consuming the communion of the Savior's body and blood but not having the understandings mentioned in this chapter, there will still be damnation and sickness among believers. If we do not understand we are actually consuming his body, which is food for our spirits, and that his blood is the blood of the new, everlasting covenant, it is like not having these benefits at all and still living under pre-resurrection experiences. It would benefit the enemy of your soul (Satan) to issue a fear-based, false generational doctrine, especially if he knew it feeds your spirit and helps you experience the benefits of the New Covenant—and more important, if it keeps from experiencing intimacy with God. This fear-based, false generational system of teachings about the communion is a doctrine of devils, as described in 1 Timothy 4:1. "Now the Spirit speaketh expressly, that in the latter times some shall depart from the faith, giving heed to seducing spirits, and doctrines of devils" (KJV).

The Communion Fast is a concept that was downloaded to me, and I was hesitant to share in this book, but I think it will benefit a lot of people. It is true as explained in the previous chapter, "The Benefits of Fasting and Prayer," that fasting is actually abstaining from food. With the communion fast, you would include it into your time of fasting. The concept is to consume nothing but the communion while fasting. You can start by taking communion at the beginning and the end of your time of fasting. Then eventually consume nothing but the sacraments during your entire time of fasting. The amounts are so small that the impact of food consumption is very minimal. The intent is to combine the power of fasting with the power of the communion. Fasting disciplines the body and realigns your being, while his communion feeds your spirit. As Yeshua stated in John 6:55, "For my body is real food for your spirit" (TPT). As with any dietary changes, always consult your physician.

Chapter Reflections and Notes

chapter seventeen

The Conclusion and Final Instructions

In conclusion, I eagerly suggest that you implement what you have discovered in this book into your life. I also leave you with an invitation from God, the lover of your soul, and some final words and instructions.

An Invitation From God, the Lover of Your Soul

Listen! Are you thirsty for more? Come to the refreshing waters (me) and drink. Even if you have no money, come, buy, and eat. Yes, come and buy all the wine and milk you desire—it won't cost a thing. Why spend your hard-earned money on something that can't nourish you or work so hard for something that can't satisfy? So, listen carefully to me and you'll enjoy a sumptuous feast, delighting in the finest of food. Pay attention and come closer to me, and hear, that your total being may flourish. I will enter into an everlasting covenant with you, and I will show you the same faithful love that I showed David. See! I made him a witness to the nations, an example of leadership, as prince and commander of peoples." Look! You will summon nations you've never heard of. Nations who have never heard of you will come running to follow you because Yahweh, your God, the Holy One of Israel, has glorified (honored) you! (Isaiah 55:1–5 TPT)

Love has a developmental process that God uses to authenticate the love inside of us and for us. That process connects to our relationship with him. Again, all these relationships must be not just experienced but also felt. The scriptures record, "If someone says, 'I love God,' and hates [the opposite of love] his brother, he is a liar; for he who does not love his brother whom he has seen, how can he love God whom he has not seen?" (1 John 4:20 NKJV).

It is a process that starts horizontally with other people and then develops into the vertical connection in your relationship with God, the lover of your soul. Now, I know some of you may be saying this is a tricky thing. I may not know the people in your life, but I do know that as long as the relationships are not abusive and toxic, God can help you with this. He will not allow other people to be the thing that stands in the way of you and him. He will speed up the process and do whatever is necessary to get to you. But you must remember you are only responsible for your actions in love and not of anyone else's. Keep the Bible's definition of love and not your own.

Love is large and incredibly patient. Love is gentle and consistently kind to all. It refuses to be jealous when blessing comes to someone else. Love does not brag about one's achievements nor inflate its own importance. Love does not traffic in shame and disrespect, nor selfishly seek its own honor. Love is not easily irritated or quick to take offense. Love joyfully celebrates honesty and finds no delight in what is wrong. Love is a safe place of shelter, for it never stops believing the best for others. Love never

takes failure as defeat, for it never gives up.
(1 Corinthians 13:4–7 TPT)

I know for some this process will be complicated due to your relationship experiences. The takeaway is to forgive and be responsible for your love. Ask God, the lover of your soul, for help and he will help you through this process. Be diligent not to put God in the same category as those who you see and experience. For he is not like humankind. He is not just capable of loving you with a love that is unimaginable, but his entire being is love. "Those who are loved by God, let his love continually pour from you to one another, because God is love. Everyone who loves is fathered by God and experiences an intimate knowledge of him" (1 John 4:7 TPT).

Final Instructions

Here is the adventure to deeper intimacy with God, the lover of your soul.

1. Examine your faith at least once a year—the more often, the better. Ask yourself, "What do I believe? How do I view God? Do I see him as the lover of my soul?" You must believe that a deep, intimate

relationship with God is possible—one that cannot only be experienced but also felt. Recognize that you will never have anyone else want you this much and in this way.

2. Look at the natural relationships you have had in your life. Whether personal or the ones from observation, if they are good, use them as examples. If you unfortunately do not have any models, look around at others in your life. Realize that relationships grow in time. Let this journey with God happen fluidly and naturally. The quality of time spent versus the quantity of time spent will eventually produce more time spent. These times include prayer, reading, and meditating on the Word of God. When two people are interested in each other, no one has to schedule time to spend with each other. It is something they naturally and eagerly want to do. It is the same thing with God, the lover of your soul.

3. The chapter "The Secret Place" in this book about the secret place offers a unique approach to developing intimacy with God, the lover of your soul. Revisiting it would be a good idea. Finding your secret place or places is even better.

4. Start somewhere in the area of fasting. If it has to be only an hour, so be it, but then start to increase

the amount of time and days. The key is to fast with understanding and instructions you have gained from the following chapters: "The Purpose and Benefits of Fasting and Prayer," "The Communion Revelation," and the communion fast.

5. The twenty-one-day total submersion: Focus on one thing for twenty-one days, implementing the previous instructions mentioned in this chapter. Let God, the lover of your soul, be the first initial focus of your first twenty-one-day submersion. Then change focus to another topic. Revisit the chapters in this book, your reflections, and your notes during these times.

6. Share and connect: Share your experiences with those in your sphere of influence and connection! Share with your family and friends what you have learned and discovered on this new adventure to find a deeper intimacy with God, the lover of your soul! Post about it on your social media accounts. Lastly, connect with us as we all travel on this new adventure of discovering a deeper intimacy with God. I want to lock hands with you and create an eternal heavenly connection. I want us to walk step by step through this new adventure together and discover what it

really means to "love God [the lover of your soul] with all ... your soul" (Matthew 22:37 NKJV).

Subscribe. Stay Connected & Informed at:
GodTheLoverOfYourSoul.com

Chapter Reflections and Notes

Bibliography and Appendix

1. "Black Box." Radiolab. https://www.radiolab.org/story/black-box/.
2. Charles Darwin, *On the Origin of Species* (Broadview Press).
3. D. A. Dewitt, *History of Life Course ePack* (Creation Curriculum).
4. "Explore 4 Different Types of Love in the Bible," Learn Religions, December 15, 2010, https://www.learnreligions.com/types-of-love-in-the-bible-700177.
5. M. Gershon, *The Second Brain: The Scientific Basis of Gut Instinct and a Groundbreaking New Understanding of Nervous Disorders of the Stomach and Intestine* (Harper, 1998).
6. *Merriam-Webster's Collegiate Dictionary*, 11th ed.
7. L. Stannard, "What Parts of the Human Brain Correspond to Emotion or Love?" *Livestrong*, April 2019, https://www.livestrong.com/

article/77419-parts-human-brain-correspond-emotion/.

8. "Strong's Greek: 1271. διάνοια (dianoia)—The Mind, Disposition, Thought," Bible Hub, https://biblehub.com/greek/1271.htm.

9. "Strong's Greek: 2588. καρδία (kardia)—Heart," Bible Hub, https://biblehub.com/greek/2588.htm.

10. *Strong's Greek: 5590. ψυχή (psuché)—Breath, the Soul,"* Bible Hub, https://biblehub.com/greek/5590.htm.

11. E. Underhill, *Mysticism: A Study in the Nature and Development of Man's Spiritual Consciousness*, 8th ed. (Aeterna Press, 2015).

12. N. Webster, *Webster's 1828 American Dictionary of the English Language* (Waking Lion, 2015).

13. "What Kind of Love Is Philia in the Bible?" Learn Religions, December 15, 2010, https://www.learnreligions.com/what-is-philia-700691.

14. R. F. Youngblood and T. N. Publishers, *Nelson's New Illustrated Bible Dictionary* (Thomas Nelson, 2000).

Resources:

Visit Dr. William Lane Craig, at www.reasonablefaith.org

Visit Answer In Genesis at www.answersingenesis.org/answers

What is the meaning of life?

Why am I here?

https://youtu.be/NKGnXgH_CzE

Does God (The Creator) even exist? What about evolution?

https://youtu.be/EE76nwimuT0

https://youtu.be/ChWiZ3iXWwM

https://youtu.be/CFYswvGoaPU

https://youtu.be/fk1pEHXnPsE

https://youtu.be/Qi7ANgO2ZBU

Why should I believe in Jesus (Yeshua) or the Bible? What about the other faiths?

https://patternsofevidence.com

https://youtu.be/RRyq6RwzlEM

https://youtu.be/kWSG5okmUr8

Printed in the United States
by Baker & Taylor Publisher Services

Printed in the United States
by Baker & Taylor Publisher Services